"You Can Have What You Say!"

Kenneth E. Hagin

25 And a certain woman, which had an issue of blood twelve years,

26 And had suffered many things of many physicians, and had spent all that she had, and was nothing bettered, but rather grew worse,

27 When she had heard of Jesus, came in the press behind, and touched his garment.

28 For she said, If I may touch but his clothes, I shall be whole.

29 And straightway the fountain of her blood was dried up; and she felt in her body that she was healed of that plague.

30 And Jesus, immediately knowing in himself that virtue had gone out of him, turned him about in the press, and said, Who touched my clothes?

31 And his disciples said unto him, Thou seest the multitude thronging thee, and sayest thou, Who touched me?

32 And he looked round about to see her that had done this thing.

33 But the woman fearing and trembling, knowing what was done in her, came and fell down before him, and told him all the truth.

34 And he said unto her, Daughter, thy faith hath made thee whole; go in peace, and be whole of thy plague.

CHAPTER 1

You Can Have What You Say

You can have what you say.

The woman who touched Jesus' garment received exactly what she said. The Bible says, **"For she said,** *If I may touch but his clothes, I shall be whole"* (v. 28).

What she said was her faith speaking. I know it was, for Jesus said, *"Daughter, thy faith hath made thee whole"* (v. 34).

What you say is your faith speaking. **You can have what you say.**

MARK 11:23-24

23 For verily I say unto you, That whosoever shall say unto this mountain, Be thou removed, and be thou cast into the sea; and shall not doubt in his heart, but shall believe that those things which he saith shall come to pass; he shall have whatsoever he saith.

24 Therefore I say unto you, What things soever ye desire, when ye pray, believe that ye receive them, and ye shall have them.

We are using the last clause of Mark 11:23 as our text: *"He shall have whatsoever he saith."*

Another wonderful proof text is found in the Old Testament. Numbers 13 tells us that after the children of Israel reached Kadesh-Barnea, they sent 12 spies into Canaan. Ten of the spies brought back an evil report from the Promised Land, and two brought back a good report.

What is an evil report? It is a report of doubt.

What is a good report? It is a report of faith.

Ten of them said, "It's true, all right, that the land is flowing with milk and honey." They even displayed the giant clusters of grapes, pomegranates, and other fruit they had brought back from Canaan. "But," they warned, "there are giants in the land. And in our eyes we are as grasshoppers in their sight."

When you analyze their report, they were saying, "We can't do it. We can't take the land." And all of Israel accepted this report. (Some people believe the majority report is always right, but if you follow the majority of Christians—even Full Gospel Christians—you will walk in unbelief.) By accepting the majority report, the children of Israel were saying, "We can't take the land."

You can have what you say. The children of Israel got exactly what they said. They believed they couldn't take it, so they said they couldn't take it. And they didn't.

After all, even when you doubt, you believe *something;* you just believe the wrong thing. That is the only difference.

You always get and have in your life what you believe for and say. If you do not believe what you are saying, you should not say it, because if you say something long enough, those words eventually will register on your spirit and will control your life.

Each one of those ten spies got exactly what he said. Not one of them entered the Promised Land. They all wandered in the wilderness until they died. What they said came to pass.

It was different for Joshua and Caleb. Caleb said, *"Let us go up at once, and possess it; for we are well able to overcome it"* (Num. 13:30). Joshua said, *"Only rebel not ye against the Lord, neither fear ye the people of the land; for they are bread for us: their defence is departed from them, and the Lord is with us: fear them not"* (Num. 14:9).

Joshua and Caleb did not deny that there were giants in the land. "Yes," they admitted, "in our own eyes we are as grasshoppers in their sight." But when you analyze what they said, they confessed, "Our God is well able to deliver them into our hands. We're well able to overcome the giants and possess the land."

People often come to me asking, "Will you tell me why I can't get healed?"

I always smile and say, "Yes."

Their eyes get big and they say, "Well, if you can, I wish you would."

I say, "You just got through telling me you can't."

You can have what you say. Their words give them away. You can locate people by what they say. Their confession locates them.

When I pray for people, I try to get a confession from them before I pray for them.

I ask them, "Will you be healed now as I lay my hands on your head and pray?"

"Well, Brother Hagin, I—I—I sure *hope* I will."

And I always have to say, "Well, you won't. You won't."

You see, I've located them. I know where they are now. They're not in faith. They're in *hope.*

"Will you be filled with the Holy Spirit now as I lay my hands upon your head and pray?" I ask them.

"Well, I sure *hope* I will, Brother Hagin."

And I always have to say, "Well, you won't be." I've located them.

Those who have a quick confession of faith receive almost instantly.

Some people, however, think that because I preach this way, they can just say it out of their heads without believing it in their hearts. I have noticed that these people do not look me in the eye when they say it, and I detect a note of hesitancy in their voice. That little hesitancy will defeat them.

It's the little foxes, the Bible says, that spoil the vine (Song of Sol. 2:15). It's not some great big something that's keeping most of God's children from being healed or filled with the Spirit.

It wasn't the giants in Canaan who kept Israel from entering in. If it had been the giants, they would have defeated Joshua and Caleb, just as they did the rest of the spies. No, the 10 spies defeated themselves. It was their wrong thinking, wrong believing, and wrong talking that defeated them.

It is not the giants in life who defeat people. It is not the storms of life that defeat you. It is not the devil who defeats you. If you are defeated, you have defeated yourself by your wrong thinking, wrong believing, and wrong talking.

Joshua and Caleb said, "Our God is well able to deliver them into our hands. We are well able to overcome them."

You can have what you say.

The woman with the issue of blood got exactly *what she said.*

Those Israelites who accepted the majority report got exactly *what they said:* They wandered in the wilderness until every one of them died.

Joshua and Caleb were the only members of that generation who entered the Promised Land. Joshua became the leader, and when they got into Canaan, Caleb came to Joshua and said, "Give me this mountain!" (Joshua 14:12). (Oh, I like this fellow Caleb. I like a man of faith. Caleb has a special place in my heart.)

I think Joshua looked back 40 years and realized that he and Caleb had won a victory in believing and talking right. He wanted to locate Caleb, so he asked him (to get a confession out of him), "Are you able to take the mountain? There are giants in the mountain. The Anakims are in that mountain."

And old Caleb said, in effect, "I am well able. I am 85 years old, but my natural strength is not abated. My eyesight is not even dim. I am well able to take the mountain." And bless God, he did!

—CHAPTER 2—

Don't Prepare for Failure

Many things happen because we think they *ought* to happen.

Recently I read about a scientist who says that after you reach a certain age, it becomes more difficult for your brain to remember things. When I got past 40, I found I could not remember scriptures as well as I once did. After a while, I said to myself, "There's no need for this. After all, the brain is simply a physical organ that the mind operates through. The mind is part of my inward being—and the mind never grows old." (The rich man in hell still had his mind and memory intact, because Abraham said in Luke 16:25, "Son, remember . . .")

The moment I started believing, thinking, and talking right, I could quote all the scriptures I ever quoted. I could remember everything just as easily as ever—and my memory actually got better instead of worse!

We fail many times because we get ready to fail. We prepare for failure. We think it, believe it, and do it. But we as believers should never talk failure, doubt, or unbelief. We should talk faith.

If you are defeated, you are defeated with your own lips.

I appreciate and thank God for all the good material in print today on this subject, but years ago I got the secret from the text quoted earlier, where Jesus said:

MARK 11:23-24

23 For verily I say unto you, That whosoever shall say unto this mountain, Be thou removed, and be thou cast into the sea; and shall not doubt in his heart, but shall believe that those things which he saith shall come to pass; he shall have whatsoever he saith.

24 Therefore I say unto you, What things soever ye desire, when ye pray, believe that ye receive them, and ye shall have them.

In 1933, I was just a boy of 16 lying on a bed of sickness. Four months before I turned 16 I had become totally bedfast.

Five doctors, including one who had practiced at the famous Mayo Clinic, were on my case.

I lived with my grandparents. Although my grandfather had quite a lot of property, he was not a rich man, for it was during the Great Depression. Nevertheless, if Mayo Clinic could have helped me, he would have been willing to send me there.

My doctors advised the family to listen to the doctor who had practiced at Mayo Clinic, for he was considered one of the best in America, and he knew as much as the doctors at Mayo Clinic.

He and the other attending physicians said there was no hope for me. In fact, he said I didn't have chance in a million to live. He added that as far as medical science knew, no one with my heart condition had ever lived past the age of 16.

I had never had a normal childhood. I had never run and played like other children. I had been a semi-invalid all of my life.

The town I lived in, McKinney, Texas, 32 miles north of Dallas, was the county seat of Collin County. At that time, it had a population of about 8,750. Grandpa owned several houses there and decided to move out of one into another. He had it painted and redecorated, and on New Year's Day 1934, we moved.

The movers moved furniture from other parts of the house first, leaving the furniture in my bedroom until last. Then, as they came to load it, an ambulance was called to move me.

Mr. Harris of the Harris Funeral Home, and his driver, Mr. MacDonald, lifted me off the bed onto the stretcher, carried me out, and put me in the ambulance. As we drove off, Mr. Harris turned to me and said, "Son, they tell me you've been bedfast for a year."

"No," I said, "not quite a year. About nine months."

He said, "Well, if you feel up to it, we could ride very slowly through the residential area of town, since you haven't seen it in such a long time."

Although I was partially paralyzed, I could move my head and look out. After being bedfast for nearly a year, staring at four walls and a ceiling, I thought the town looked good, even though I was looking at it out of ambulance windows.

Mr. Harris then said, "Son, if you'd like, we also could drive across the town square. It's New Year's Day, and most of the businesses are closed, so there will be very little traffic."

I said, "I'd appreciate that!"

I shall never forget it as long as I live, now and even through eternity. As I looked at that old courthouse, the devil said to me, "Well, you never did think you would ever see that building in the flesh again. And you wouldn't have, if it hadn't been for the kindness of Mr. Harris."

I knew it was the devil. Some people can't tell whether it's the devil or God talking to them, but let me tell you how you can tell the difference. *Everything that is of doubt, unbelief, and discouragement is the devil.* God never talks doubt, failure, unbelief, or discouragement to anybody. This Baptist boy had been reading his grandma's "Methodist" Bible. I remembered a verse of scripture. And something on the inside of me spoke up and brought that scripture to my remembrance: *"He shall have whatsoever he saith."*

Believe it in your heart; say it with your mouth. That is the principle of faith. **You can have what you say.**

I said it in that ambulance that day as the tears coursed down my face. I didn't understand all I know now. I just had one little gleam of light—like the light that might creep through the crack under a door—but I knew it was there. So I said it.

I said, "Yes, I will see these buildings. I will see this courthouse. I will come and stand on this courthouse square, because Jesus said, 'What you believe in your heart and say with your mouth will come to pass.' I believe it in my heart. I say it with my mouth."

About 2 o'clock in the afternoon that first day of January 1934 was the starting point with me.

Once you have committed yourself, you are located. I refused to go back on my confession of faith. January went by. I was still bedfast. February went by. I was still bedfast. March, April, May, June, July went by—seven months and I was still bedfast.

The devil kept telling me, "It's not working!" I told him, "I'm not going to believe you, you old doubter." I held fast to my confession. I refused to give it up. I said, "That scripture is what Jesus said when He was here on the earth."

I kept telling Jesus, God, the Holy Spirit, the angels, the devil, and evil spirits, "I'm going to hold fast to it." I told God, "If it doesn't work, it will be because Your Word has failed under me. I'm standing on it. Jesus and I will have to go down together, because I'm not going to turn Him loose."

On the second Saturday of August 1934, I walked to that courthouse square.

Back there in north central Texas in those Depression days of 1934, everybody, particularly all the country folks, always came to town on Saturday. There were so many people there that I had to elbow my way through the crowd to get to the curb. But I stood on that curb, on the southeast corner where the grocery store was, and tears rolled their way down my face. I lifted my hand, and I didn't care what people thought. That's one thing I've never been bothered with.

I said, "Devil, I told you so!" And I said, "Devil, I don't know whether you can read or not, but in case you can't . . ." I pulled my New

Testament out of my shirt pocket, opened it to Mark 11:23–24, and read it to him.

I said, "I told you it would work all of those months you told me it wasn't working, and wouldn't work, and wasn't going to work. I told you it was the Word of God. And here it is."

I don't know what people thought, seeing a 17-year-old boy standing on that street corner with a Testament in his hands, tears rolling down his face, talking to somebody. But I did not care. I had begun to hold fast to this scripture on my bed of sickness, and I've been holding fast to it ever since.

—Chapter 3—

A Boy Preacher's Vision

So I began my ministry. I finished school and became a Baptist boy preacher, pastoring a community church eight miles out in the country from that courthouse square.

The first year I preached, I wore out four pairs of shoes walking to church—and I didn't get enough money to buy one pair. I didn't have a car. If somebody picked me up, well and good, but most of the time I would walk, and many times I walked at least five miles of the distance to the church.

I want to tell you, I had a hilarious time preaching the Gospel. I knew, you see, that **you can have what you say**. It had brought me out of the bed of sickness. It had healed me of heart trouble and paralysis, and it had given me health. So I knew Jesus saved. I knew Jesus healed. I knew Jesus was coming again. I didn't know then about His baptizing in the Holy Spirit.

I would walk down that dusty road, saying, "I'll preach that Jesus saves, and Jesus heals, and that Jesus is coming again. And I'll preach it from the Red River to the Gulf of Mexico. I'll preach it from the Louisiana border to the New Mexico state line." (I thought if I covered Texas that would be doing pretty good!) I said I would do it, because I knew I could have what I said.

Then I began associating with Full Gospel people, because they believed in divine healing like I did. They also preached something else: being filled with the Holy Spirit and speaking with other tongues.

Like one man said, "It's sort of like a slippery creek bank. You keep fooling around and you'll slip in." I kept fooling around, and I slipped in.

I continued to preach the same thing I had been preaching—except I added a little to it. That's one thing that the baptism in the Holy Spirit will do for you: it will enlarge your vision!

Walking down that road to church, I began saying, "I'll preach the Gospel. I'll preach that Jesus saves. I'll preach that Jesus heals. I'll preach that He fills with the Holy Spirit. I'll preach that He's coming again." Only now I added, "I'll preach it from the Atlantic to the Pacific. I'll preach it from Los Angeles to New York. I'll preach it from the Gulf of Mexico to the Canadian border." Praise God, the Holy Spirit will give you a bigger vision than Texas! And bless God, I've done it. I've traveled hundreds of thousands of miles in the United States and Canada and even overseas telling the story that **you can have what you say**.

When my wife, Oretha, and I married in November of 1938, she was Methodist and knew nothing about divine healing. In December the first real norther blew in, and she took a bad throat.

She said, "I've got to go have my throat swabbed. I'll have a bad throat all winter. I do every year."

This was a good opportunity to teach her. Remembering Mark 11:23 I turned to her and said, "No, we'll not have your throat swabbed. That chronic sore throat will leave you and will never come back."

It left. And these years have come and gone and it's never come back. **You can have what you say.**

When I went on the evangelistic field in 1949, we rented an apartment. My father-in-law died in 1950, and I promised him on his deathbed, "Don't you worry about Mrs. Rooker (my mother-in-law). She'll have a home with us. We'll take care of her." She came to live with us in that apartment, but when I came home, I didn't have any place to sleep. So I said to my wife, "There's no need for us to live in this little apartment. Let's get a house."

At first we rented a three-bedroom frame house. Then I said, "We could buy this house, and the payment would be much cheaper than rent." We agreed, and I asked my wife to see if the owner would sell it. The owner replied, "No, we won't sell it. We built it for our own home, and we plan to move back there someday."

I wrote my wife, "Well, they want to sell it; they just don't know what they're talking about, because Jesus said, 'You can have what you say.' And that house is mine."

The next time I was home, I went outside, walked around the yard, and prayed, "You said every place the sole of your foot shall tread upon shall be yours (Joshua 1:3). My feet have trod upon it. It's mine."

After a short interval, I said, "Ask her again." The owner replied again, "No, no. We don't want to sell." I wrote my wife, "Yes, they want to sell it. They just don't know it. That place is mine."

In the process of time, the owner said to my wife, "We have decided to sell the house." When my wife told me, I said, "It's no news to me. I've known it for months."

We made an appointment to see the owners, but we learned that somebody else wanted to give them $500 more for the house, and it was worth it. Sitting in their home, I told the owners, "I certainly would hate for you folks to miss God."

The woman said to her husband, "Tell them what you told me the last three nights."

He said, "You tell them."

She said, "Well, we pray before we go to bed, and each night as we got into bed, my husband has said, 'You know, something on the inside of me tells me that house belongs to that preacher. It's his house.' "

I said, "Sure it does. It's my house."

Praise God, **you can have what you say**. I'm still saying it.

We got the house. I had been paying $80 a month rent, but my payment after refinancing was only about $56, and the house now belonged to me. **You can have what you say.**

I remember, too, that the first year I was on the evangelistic field, the devil tried to shut off my finances. After the first year was over, I would have been $1,200 better off in cash if I had stayed with the church I had pastored. In addition, the church furnished us with a parsonage and paid all our utility bills. Now I had to furnish my family with a place to live as well as pay for my traveling expenses.

By the end of that year, I had to sell my old car to try to get enough money to pay the interest on three loans I had.

I said, "Lord, something's wrong somewhere. I'm in Your will. I'm doing what You told me to do. If there was any doubt at all about it, I would go back to pastoring."

And I said, "You said in Your Word, 'If you be willing and obedient, you shall eat the good of the land' (Isa. 1:19). I know that if you want us to eat the good, you want us to drive the good—the best. Here I've had to sell my automobile."

And the Lord said, "That text said, 'If you are willing and obedient.' You are obedient, but you have not been willing."

I got willing in a hurry. I said to Him, "Now I'm willing, and You know I'm willing. I've made an adjustment."

He said, "Yes, you are willing, but another trouble with you is that you don't practice what you preach."

I considered that a low blow. I said, "Why, Lord, what do You mean I don't practice what I preach?"

"Oh," He said, "you preach faith, but you don't practice faith."

I said, "What do you mean?"

He said, "When it comes to healing you do. You have always been healed, and your children have always received healing. Even when something is wrong with your body or you have symptoms, you will get right up and declare that you are healed. And it has never failed. But the principles of faith are the same in the realm of finances as they are in the realm of healing."

I said, "Thank You. Bless God, I'm going to buy a car. A good one."

I said to my wife, "I'm going to buy a car." I told her what the Lord said.

She said, "It looks like the silliest thing in the world for us to go buy an automobile and take on an $80-a-month payment when we haven't been meeting our budget. We haven't even been making the payments we've got to make."

When you act presumptuously, you will fall flat on your face and the devil will defeat you and defeat you badly. But when you act because you have a foundation of God's Word under you, you will defeat the devil in every combat.

The easiest thing we ever did in our life was to pay for that car. It wasn't a brand-new one. We bought it from a pastor. It was a 1949 Oldsmobile Dynamic 88 with only a few miles on it.

After it was nearly worn out, I began confessing, "I'm going to buy a new car." I told every pastor where I preached, "In October, when I get to Fort Worth, the new cars will be out, and I'm going to buy a new car."

When I got to Fort Worth and started a meeting, I told the pastor, "I'm going to buy a new car while I'm here." And God is my witness that I couldn't have bought an old setting hen, looking at it from the natural standpoint.

My Oldsmobile had 93,000 miles on it by that time. It had done a wonderful job for me, so I said, "I'm going to buy an Oldsmobile. Only this time I'm going to buy an Oldsmobile 98. I want the best one. I want power brakes, power steering, air-conditioning—everything on it."

The pastor said, "Well, I know a car dealer who has one, and he always gives preachers a good deal. We'll go see him."

The next day or so, we drove down that way. As we rode along, I told the pastor all the features I wanted on the car.

As we drove up, he said, "There it sits, right there."

I said, "Bless God, that's even the color I had in mind."

I looked it over, and I said, "Yes, this is the one I want. This is it."

We went into the office, and the pastor introduced me to the car dealer, who was a sinner man. This pastor had known the man for years. The car dealer was sitting there with his feet propped up on his desk. He had a big, black cigar in his mouth. The pastor said, "Mr. So-and-So, this is Brother Hagin. He's holding a meeting for us. He's interested in that new Oldsmobile sitting out there."

The fellow looked out the window, swung his feet down off the desk, and said, "Yeah, you can have it if you want it, any way you want it."

He said, "I carry my own notes. I'll carry your note three full years and put a big balloon note on the end of the three years if you want me to. I believe every preacher ought to have a new car, and I'm doing my best to see that they get one."

Well, I told that car dealer what I wanted my payment to be. He started writing and said, "Sign here." He never got out of his chair even to look at my old car. And I drove away in the new one. Praise the Lord. Because **you can have what you say**. It works. Praise God, I know it works.

Somebody might say, "Yes, but you were in the ministry, and you needed a car. It would work for you." I can tell you lay members that it worked for.

This principle doesn't just work for something big. It will work for something small too.

—**CHAPTER 4**—

You Can't Outdo God

In 1954, my family and I moved to Port Arthur, Texas, on the advice of our pastor, Brother Leonard Wood. He had moved from pastoring the First Assembly of God Church in Garland to the First Assembly in Port Arthur. He and his wife sort of looked after my family while I was away preaching—and I was gone 85 percent of the time or more.

He said, "My wife and your wife are like sisters, and we help her. Why don't you move down here?

"I've been thinking about it," I said.

Later we went out to eat with one of the church members and started talking about it again. The church member mentioned a friend who wanted to sell his house.

Well, again, I couldn't have bought an old setting hen in the natural.

So I said, "Well, I'd rather rent it than buy it."

The church member suggested we look at the house. He introduced me to the owner and said, "Brother C., Brother Hagin is thinking about moving here from Garland, and he is interested in your house."

"I just phoned in an ad to rent it fully furnished," Brother C. explained.

"Well," I said, "I've got my own furniture."

Brother C. said, "I would rather sell the house. I'll tell you what I'll do, Brother Hagin. Some members of the church have offered me so much for the house, but I'll sell it to you for $750 less than what they offered. And I'll sell it to you for $1,000 down. I'll carry the note myself at so much a month. That garage apartment is rented to Full Gospel people, and the rent on it will almost make the payment for you."

I started to say, "Well, I don't have $1,000. I can't borrow $1,000." But I happened to remember this scripture.

I remembered **you can have what you say**.

I said, "All right. I'm saying it: Brother C., I will have $1,000 for you in 10 days."

"Fine," he said. "Do you want to consider it sold?"

"Certainly," I said. I had really put myself on the spot.

But do you know what happened? The next day, the telephone rang in the parsonage, and Brother Wood said it was for me. I went to the phone and a woman said, "Is this Brother Hagin?"

"Yes," I said.

"This is Sister E.," she said. "Do you remember me?"

"Yes."

"Well," she said, "I was praying last night, and God told me to give you $500 and to loan you $500."

I said, "I don't doubt it, sister. Bring it on over."

She came by the parsonage and handed me an envelope. It had ten $100 bills in it.

Hallelujah to Jesus, you can't outdo God. If you will just believe and act on His Word, **you can have what you say**.

Let me give you this illustration in closing. My wife and I took our little niece Ruth into our home when she was 15. My sister's home was broken, and my sister had to go to work. Left alone, my niece got into the wrong company, so we took her in.

She was saved and filled with the Holy Spirit after she had been with us about a month. She began to teach Sunday School, because she had such a burden to work with children.

After she was graduated from high school, she went to work. Then my sister, who had remarried, moved to our town, and Ruth moved back home to live.

Ruth got out of church for a while. She met a young man where she worked, and married him. She told him, "I'm not in fellowship with God exactly, but I believe in speaking in tongues." He was a Baptist, but he pretended it was all right.

Just as soon as they were married, however, he said, "I'm the head of this house, and you're not going around any of those tongue-talkers. That's the end of it." He treated us very coolly.

Ruth and Benny were living in Houston, and we were living in Port Arthur. One morning about 5 o'clock, the telephone rang. It was long distance. The woman on the other end was almost in hysterics. I couldn't understand who it was.

Finally I said, "Who is it? Who is it?" It was my sister. I said, "Either be quiet or talk so that I can understand you."

"Well," she said, "Ruth's baby was born, and they wouldn't let Benny or anybody see him. In fact, the doctor said the baby was born dead. Then the doctor returned and said, 'The baby isn't dead as we thought, but he will die. He can't live. And it would be best that none of the family ever sees him, because his head and face are all deformed.'"

She said, "Benny wanted me to telephone you and ask you to pray."

I said, "Now, Oleta, *'whosoever shall say and shall not doubt in his heart, but shall believe that those things which he saith shall come to pass; he shall have whatsoever he saith.'* The minute you hang up this phone, you turn and say, 'Benny, Uncle Ken said the baby will live and not die, and he will be all right.'"

"Oh, Ken, do you think so?" she said.

I said, "No, I don't think so. I know so."

She said, "He wanted me to phone and have you pray. Are you going to pray?"

"No," I said. "I'm not going to pray. There's no use to pray. I've already said it. Jesus said, 'You will have whatsoever you say.'"

"Well," she said, "Ruth wants Oretha to come."

I said, "I've got a day service, and I can't take her, but I'll get somebody else to take her."

Oretha and a friend arrived in Houston about 10 o'clock that morning. Benny ran down the steps of the hospital, threw his arms around my wife, hugged her, and said, "I'm a Pentecostal Baptist! I'm a Pentecostal Baptist! I'm a Pentecostal Baptist!"

He said, "Uncle Ken hadn't hung up that phone 10 minutes until the nurses came rushing out saying, 'You can see the baby now! He's all right. While we were standing looking at him, his head filled out as if it were a balloon being blown up. And he's all right. He's going to live.'"

You should see that boy today. He's a big fellow. And you should see Benny today. Praise God, he *is* a Pentecostal Baptist, filled with the Holy Spirit and speaking with other tongues.

Praise God, you can have what you say.